ECONOMY
AND
SOCIETY

WILBERT E. MOORE
Princeton University

UBLEDAY SHORT STUDIES IN SOCIOLOGY

Economy and Society

DOUBLEDAY SHORT STUDIES IN SOCIOLOGY

Consulting Editor

Charles H. Page

Professor of Sociology, Smith College

|||||||||||||||||||||||||||||||||||||||||||||||||||||||||||||||||||||||||||||||||||||||||||||||||||||||||||||||||||||||||||||||||||||||||||||||||||||||||||||||||||||||||||||||||||||||||||

ALREADY PUBLISHED

Man in Society: Preface to Sociology and the Social Sciences by George Simpson, Assistant Professor of Sociology, Brooklyn College.

Sociological Perspective: Basic Concepts and Their Application by Ely Chinoy, Assistant Professor of Sociology, Smith College.

Social Planning in America: A Dynamic Interpretation by Joseph S. Himes, Professor of Sociology, North Carolina College at Durham.

Religion and Society by Elizabeth K. Nottingham, Assistant Professor of Sociology, Queens College.

The Development of Modern Sociology: Its Nature and Growth in the United States by Roscoe C. Hinkle Jr., Assistant Professor of Sociology, University of Rochester, and Gisela J. Hinkle, Lecturer in Sociology, University of Rochester.

Interpreting Social Change in America by Norman F. Washburne, Assistant Professor of Sociology, Southern State College.

Economy and Society by Wilbert E. Moore, Professor of Sociology, Princeton University.

Language and Society by Joseph Bram, Professor of Sociology and Anthropology, New York University.

FORTHCOMING

Social Organization by Scott A. Greer, Research Director, Laboratory in Urban Culture, Occidental College.

Class and Society by Kurt B. Mayer, Associate Professor of Sociology, Brown University.

Community and Its Study by Alfred P. Parsell, Assistant Professor of Sociology and Anthropology, City College of New York.

Sociology and Social Work by Arthur Hillman, Professor of Sociology and Chairman of the Department, Roosevelt University.

Science as a Social Institution by Gerald De Gré, Associate Professor of Sociology, Bard College.

Racial and Ethnic Groups by John H. Burma, Professor of Sociology and Chairman of the Department, Grinnell College.

Bureaucracy in Modern Society by Peter M. Blau, Assistant Professor of Sociology, University of Chicago.

Twentieth Century Rural America by Lewis W. Jones, Director of Research, Rural Life Council, Tuskegee Institute.

Social Movements by C. Wendell King, Assistant Professor of Sociology, University of Massachusetts.

Population: Society's Human Resources by Dennis H. Wrong, Research Associate, Department of Political Economy, University of Toronto.

Men and Their Cities by Ira de A. Reid, Professor of Sociology and Chairman of the Department, Haverford College.

Social Control of Disturbing Behavior by Richard D. Schwartz, Instructor in Sociology, Yale University.

To order these titles and to receive forthcoming ones (none more than 95c), enter your subscription now. All titles will be sent on approval. COLLEGE DEPARTMENT, Doubleday & Company, Inc., 575 Madison Avenue, New York 22, N.Y.

Doubleday Short Studies in Sociology

Economy and Society

By WILBERT E. MOORE,
Princeton University

DOUBLEDAY & COMPANY, INC.

Garden City, N.Y.

1955

COVER ILLUSTRATION—A reproduction of a photograph
of Henry Moore's "The Family Group."
— Collection The Museum of Modern Art, New York
— A. Conger Goodyear Fund

LIBRARY OF CONGRESS CATALOG CARD NUMBER 54–12454
PRINTED IN THE UNITED STATES OF AMERICA
AT THE COUNTRY LIFE PRESS, GARDEN CITY, N.Y.

Editor's Foreword

‖‖

For several decades a *disciplinary* division of labor has provided the principal basis for specialization in social science. However, conceptual theory
and related empirical research as well as curricular organization today are
marked by a growing emphasis upon interdisciplinary and "integrated" projects. This development is in part a reaction against overspecialization; at
times it seems to reject the established disciplines themselves. But effective
interdisciplinary pursuits, in theory and research and in the classroom, require knowledge of the nature, the accumulated accomplishments, and the
limitations of both general and special sciences of man—we cannot *integrate* from scratch. This point of view, I believe, underlies Professor
Moore's *Economy and Society*.

Different types of publications reflect the interdisciplinary trend. Thus a
number of introductory textbooks are of the omnibus variety, carrying repre-
sentatives of various social sciences who all too often ride together as intel-
lectual strangers. In contrast, fruitful intercommunication and some degree
of theoretical *rapprochement* are achieved in one or two recent volumes
that bring together contributions from sociology, cultural anthropology, and
psychology; these are works that explore the interconnections between socio-
cultural structure and personality in an effort to build an integrated theory
of human behavior. But on the level of institutional analysis, cooperative
endeavors between sociologists on the one hand and historians, political
scientists, and economists on the other are largely confined to researches
on special problems. The overlapping contours of these disciplines, their
already realized and many potential contributions to one another, their
dynamic roles in an inclusive social science—these are matters neglected for
the most part or treated superficially in current publications. One phase of
this situation is redressed by Professor Moore's study.

Professor Moore is concerned with relations between what modern usage
designates as "society" and "economy." These relations, as he notes, are essentially relations between the whole and a part. While the study's focus is

necessarily the economic part, the author's approach is informed by the holistic orientation of sociology. This orientation means that sociologists, ultimately, must invade the domain of economics (as well as the domains of other special disciplines)—whether they define their scientific task as the study of social relations or social action or group life or normative patterns. For none of these phenomena is excluded from the market, from business and industry and labor unions, from modes of consumption and other segments of the economic realm, as Professor Moore's informed discussion demonstrates. Moreover, the discussion includes an unusually clear treatment of problems concerning the interpretation of social change which are of great interest to both sociology and economics and indeed to social science as such.

Economy and Society, then, develops important lessons for students of sociology and anthropology, who are apt to be overly preoccupied with currently conventional disciplinary tasks or who substitute ritualistic allegiance to interrelational and holistic concepts for hard-headed study of relationships themselves; for students of economics, who frequently need to be reminded of the social and cultural aspects of economic affairs; for students of social life in general who seek realistic understanding of one of its major components. By no means incidentally, all readers of this study will find that the sociological approach itself is clarified by Professor Moore's application of it to a particular problem area.

Thus *Economy and Society* is well designed for various reading audiences. Students and instructors of introductory courses in both sociology and economics have available a highly useful work, one that no doubt also will be exploited in more advanced courses and seminars in these subjects. The study will be especially welcomed by the designers of and participants in the rapidly expanding interdisciplinary educational projects.

Though the need for a study of this order is apparent, few scholars possess the qualifications to meet it. One important reason for the high merit of Professor Moore's analysis of relations between economy and society is his knowledge of both economics and sociology; here there is no attempt to integrate from scratch. As his earlier publications, extensive researches, and many years of successful teaching testify, Professor Moore is a persistent student of both disciplines and of their theoretical and empirical interconnections. In this text, he brings out many of these interconnections succinctly.

As an early beneficiary from reading this brief but informative book and as editor of the Doubleday Short Studies in Sociology, I welcome this addition to the series. Surely all who are concerned with teaching, learning, and applying social science will join me.

CHARLES H. PAGE

Preface

The relations between Economy and Society represent, essentially, those between a part and the whole. The justifications for the division are partly conventional. In modern industrial societies there are concrete organizations and activities that are predominantly (but never exclusively) economic in their functions. It is also true that economic aspects of social behavior are the subject of a distinct social science discipline. Both of these circumstances figure prominently in this general and introductory discussion of economic affairs.

Although an attempt has been made to discuss major theoretical and empirical developments in the field, the present study cannot be regarded as definitive. Its aim is to acquaint the student and general reader with an important area of our knowledge about social life. Developments in American social organization, and in American scholarship, receive special emphasis, but broader comparative generalizations are attempted where they seem appropriate.

The title of this study is borrowed from a classic work on the sociological analysis of economic action and organization, that of Max Weber: *Wirtschaft und Gesellschaft*, Tübingen, J. C. B. Mohr, 1922. Many of the ideas are also borrowed from this outstanding sociologist.

The study represents in part a revision and expansion of an essay, "Sociology of Economic Organization," in *Twentieth Century Sociology*, edited by Georges Gurvitch and Wilbert E. Moore, and published by the Philosophical Library, Inc., New York. The publisher of the volume has kindly consented to the use of materials from that essay.

I am indebted to Betty B. Bredemeier, Managing Editor of the *Public Opinion Quarterly*, for many suggestions, both editorial and substantive.

Princeton University   WILBERT E. MOORE

Contents

chapter one

The Development of Social Economics

Within recent years an increasing number of sociologists in the United States have turned their attention to studies of the economic aspects of society and to the role of economic activity in the functioning of the social order. This area of sociological inquiry is of course scarcely a new discovery, since sociology from its inception has given at least some attention to the production and distribution of goods and services.

For a variety of reasons, most sociologists have emphasized other aspects of social structures (patterns of social action) and functions (consequences of those actions) to the virtual exclusion of the economic. Among the reasons has been the prior existence of economics, or "political economy" as it was originally known. In view of the range of data available for sociological investigation, it is not surprising that an area seemingly covered by another science should be generally neglected.

The fact that modern Western societies have provided the principal focus of empirical research and theoretical reasoning has lent a kind of spurious support to the sociologists' neglect of studies of, say, exchange and power. Those societies are themselves complex and specialized to the point of seemingly virtual autonomy of major institutional configurations like the *economy* and the *state*. If these were almost separate entities, studied by separate disciplines, sociologists could concentrate on "residual" elements of the social structure.

Some Sources in Sociology

Even prior to the developments of the last few years, however, the neglect of the economy by sociology has not been total. Especially among sociologists studying the organization of the local rural or urban community, the significance of production and distribution, of property and the division of labor, in the structure and function of communal life have been too obviously significant to be passed over. The emphasis on interrelations among the various aspects of community life has received added support in recent cultural anthropology. In both community and anthropological studies, the economic aspects of life are seen in the context of operating social systems. These two lines of development, aided by certain theoretical contributions that have tended to bridge the analytical systems of economics and sociology, have provided much of the scholarly groundwork for the great upsurge in sociological writing on aspects of "the economy" over the last two decades.

Courses now widely taught by college and university departments of sociology, like industrial sociology, were almost unknown as late as 1940. Perhaps they provide the most dramatic evidence of the sociologists' interest in the productive and distributive system. But other types of specialized research interests, and occasional courses, are in their sum almost equally impressive: occupational aspirations, mobility, and social stratification; administrative organization as it operates in business and industry; studies of industrialization and economic development in primitive and agrarian societies; business ideologies; social determinants and consequences of technological change. The list could be multiplied, but a more orderly discussion of these and related topics will comprise a major portion of the subject matter of this study.

Some Sources in Economics

Precisely because economic activity is the subject matter of a special science, developments in that field that transcend the boundaries of the "purely" economic are also likely to be of some sociological interest. At different times and in various forms there has appeared in economic writings either a recognition that economies are parts of societies and therefore presuppose certain social conditions or, more rarely, that statements about economic activity and economic relationships (that is, the body of theory) presuppose certain sociological principles relative to the structure of the social order and the nature of social cohesion.

However, the more common basis for inquiry by economists into the sociological (or at least noneconomic) aspects of production and exchange has been *empiricism,* that is, a rejection or modification of established theory on the basis of current descriptive observation. Traditional economic theory has frequently been attacked as having little relevance to the actual nature of economic activity and economic relations. Thus many attempts have been made to describe the economy "as it actually exists," relying at times upon statistics to permit some generalization. The empiricist reaction to classical theory is best exemplified in the United States by *institutionalism.* The institutional economists take into account problems of motives, norms, cultural variations, and social stratification.* The followers of the classical tradition do not.

The increasing importance of economic policy, whether on the part of government or of private concerns, has led to the employment of professional economists who are put in a position where all relevant present and predictable facts are important to decisions. But the facts cannot be derived from any single body of abstract principles nor can the determination of relevance be safely inferred from a single theoretical system. For the adviser on economic policy the sociological aspects of economic life are at least important areas of ignorance and error.

For example, will a reduction in price in a standard commodity increase the number of units sold, or actually decrease the number because potential consumers expect further reductions? Even in economic terms, more information would be required for an answer. Is the demand for the product "elastic" (strongly affected by price), as in some types of clothing, or "inelastic" (little affected by price), as in staple items of food? But additionally, one would want to know about consumers' "expectations" concerning economic trends and their own budgetary situation, their "propensity to consume" or "propensity to save." The terms in quotation marks are now a part of the language of economists. They represent an attempt by economists to take into account social and psychological factors not derivable from economic theory but appropriate to economic policy.

Other developments in the study of economics also provide sources of interest in subjects commonly studied by sociologists. Again a few examples will serve at this point, pending an orderly review of borderline areas in subsequent chapters. Labor as a factor of production consistently fails to behave according to market theory, as for example when workers do not readily change employers despite wage differences. Businessmen are often attentive to public opinion and to pressures within their organizations as well as to market forces. Consumers respond to appeals based on esthetic appearance of products and to considerations of social prestige as well as to matters of use-value and price. Each of these sets of observations tends to prompt broadening the range of theory in the field of economics. Each converts *economic man* into *social man*.

Economic Concepts and Social Theory

Economic principles, like sociological ones, hold true only within certain conditions, whether the latter are stated or unstated. This is true of any

---

* For a fuller discussion of institutionalism in American economics, see George Simpson: *Man in Society: Preface to Sociology and the Social Sciences* (Doubleday Short Studies in Sociology) New York, Doubleday & Company, Inc., 1954.

scientific principle or law. The problem with reference to economics is how seriously this limits the applicability of economic principles outside of the Western, or capitalistic, world.

The answer to this question is by no means agreed upon among scholars. One extreme view holds that economics applies only to capitalistic economies, and indeed only to such economics in stages or segments in which there are many and independent small producers. The other extreme holds that economics involves principles of human conduct wherever choice or preference is exercised, and an attempt is made to guide behavior by calculation of "net satisfactions."

Both of these views tend to "sterilize" economic science, each in a different way. The former view, that economics applies only to capitalistic economies, involves drastic time-and-place limitations when compared with the attempt to formulate general laws of social behavior. Judged by these standards, economics represents a *low* order of generalization, however abstract its principles and however applicable to early capitalistic economies. Thus, the proposition that a potential consumer of a standard product will buy at the lowest available price is subject to observational test, but only if he has some choice, which would not be true if the prices were fixed by governmental regulation, or if products are always exchanged in terms of traditional ratios. The latter view, that economics relates to universals in human conduct, involves abandonment of monetary measurement of utilities or satisfactions, and most of the technical concepts that use or imply an impersonal market for allocating resources and products. On this basis, economics represents an exceptionally *high* level of generalization, with very low descriptive relevance to the conduct of human affairs. Thus, the proposition that men will so act as to maximize their net satisfactions has *no* predictive value or possibility of observational test, without a prior specification of their values and preferences.

Classical economic theory essentially represents a model of human behavior under certain assumptions. To the extent that these assumptions are met, it is a predictive model. Where they are not met because of erroneous postulates about human motives and social organization, the model loses its utility. The applicability of the theory can be extended by working out the implications of different assumptions and varying conditions.

Very considerable strides have been made in economics toward freeing the principles governing production and exchange from the limits imposed by the assumption of "pure" capitalism. This has tended to permit the reaching of some generalizations applicable to any social system that uses a monetary basis for calculation of costs and returns, and a monetary medium for effecting exchange of goods and services. Economics no longer has to be abandoned at the physical boundaries of socialist or communist states, or the temporal boundaries of the appearance of large corporations and combinations of producers. Very much lesser strides have been made in adding substance to propositions about the exercise of choice and the maximization of net satisfactions as ways of constructively generalizing economic principles.

Much of the difficulty in generalizing economic principles is conceptual, but not simply in the sense of finding the right words. Where the phenomena are different, calling them by the same name only confuses the situation. Economic concepts like *labor, enterprise, good,* or *commodity* gain their meaning only in terms of the whole conceptual scheme of economics.* That conceptual scheme includes, prominently and essentially, the concepts of monetary measurement and market exchange.

Production in some sense goes on in all societies, and is essential for their survival. That is, the products of the natural environment are gathered, converted, and turned to human use. Food is gathered or grown; animals are killed, fleeced, or milked; wood, stone, and metals are converted to tools, weapons, ornaments, containers, or shelters. Since some specialization of roles is required, at least on the basis of age and sex, a distributive or exchange system is essential. And since all these results depend upon performance of activities by individuals, some form of labor is involved.

The essential difficulty in the concepts as applied to primitive or agrarian societies is that their "operational definition" is not the same as in a market system.[1] In a market system the operational test of labor is a financial payment for services rendered. In an agrarian society there is no such test. Of all the useful and valued activities appropriate to social existence, which constitute labor? What are the relative values of the various physical objects that result from human activities? These questions have answers where a monetary-market system prevails, but elsewhere must be approached from other directions.

It follows that discussions of "primitive economics" or "peasant village economics" commonly use concepts that are essentially metaphorical, that is, borrowed from economic theory but without precise application where the assumptions of economic theory do not hold. There is no simple solution to this conceptual problem. Where the discussion in subsequent chapters in this study relates to all societies, it must be understood that such

---

* For a general discussion on the use of concepts in sociology, see Ely Chinoy: *Sociological Perspective: Basic Concepts and Their Application* (Doubleday Short Studies in Sociology) New York, Doubleday & Company, Inc., 1954.

concepts as labor, property, and exchange are being used in a sociological sense, referring to universal social functions. They do not, at that level of generalization, permit of propositions appropriate to *economic* theory.

The conceptual problem leads to an important point in sociological theory, however. "In any society an economic activity or structure is only 'predominantly' so, as such activities or organizations cannot be concretely separated from other functions."[2] The economy is always *part* of a society, but an analytical part.

Footnotes to Chapter One

1. Moore, Wilbert E.: "The Exportability of the 'Labor Force' Concept," *American Sociological Review*, 18, No. 1:68–72 (1953).
2. *Ibid*, p. 69. See Marion J. Levy, Jr.: *The Structure of Society*, Princeton, Princeton University Press, 1952, pp. 88–98, 330–332, 389–467.

chapter two

Economic Theory and Social Norms

Perhaps the most convenient method of approaching developments in the sociological analysis of economic activity is to proceed by indirection. Many aspects of analysis left untouched or inadequately formulated by economic theory are amenable to sociological investigation. Other disciplines also impinge on the understanding of economic behavior, but the present concern is with those areas that may properly be regarded as sociological.

The indirect procedure is indicated for at least two reasons: (1) economic theory has been developed to a considerably more advanced point than have the interrelated principles of the other social sciences, and this allows a relatively greater ease in marking off the limits of competence or adequacy in existing theory; (2) correlatively, sociological theory in this as in other respects is poorly developed, and is thus difficult to summarize directly and positively. The procedure does not imply the intentional relegation of sociological analysis to those residual categories neglected by the so-called more specialized sciences.

There is a natural tendency on the part of economists to regard sociological elements in economic theory as residual, and thus possibly amenable to systematization within a broadened theoretical framework in economics. Apart from the division of scientific labor, this view is less objectionable than the view that these noneconomic elements are simply random variables as distinct from the mathematically determinate system of economic variables.

Recapitulation of "Classical" Economic Theory[1]

Classical economic theory has developed along fairly definite lines. First, economic ends or *wants* have been postulated as unlimited and random. That the ends are random means that the theory says nothing about the relations among the goals of the individual actors. This assumption has been more often implicit than explicit, as Parsons points out,[2] and has been unstable in economic theory. One notable tendency has been to "biologize" goals in one way or another—that is, to regard food, clothing, and shelter as constituting the wellsprings of human action, or at least economic action. Utility analysis attempts to provide a relationship among ends, at least in the sense of placing them in order. It does not, however, relate the ends explicitly to the normative structure of society, that is, the commonly accepted goals and rules of conduct.

Second, the actor (economic man) is postulated as having a rational orientation to his ends, that is, as relying on fact and logic in adopting the most efficient means for their achievement.

From these postulates the economist has derived the principles of maximizing utility, the calculation of alternative courses of action, and ultimately the behavior of the market. For the latter, however, certain further assumptions need to be made: the individuals act separately and not in combination, competition is (relatively) unrestricted, and the market itself is subject to no direct controls other than those imposed by the automatic operation of the pricing mechanism. Although the extreme position would assume a complete absence of external control, realization that the formulation is not only abstract but inherently unstable has generally led to the assumption of sufficient control to keep the competition fair.

This formulation is not concretely descriptive of economic affairs, and indeed cannot be. The drastically abbreviated and highly selective* statement of the subject matter of economics is sufficient to indicate several important difficulties once this type of behavior is related to the social order as a whole.

1. The "liberal" economic order assumed by the classical economists, or in fact any economic order, can only operate within certain social conditions. Those conditions include at least the minimum control necessary to regulate competition, to reduce the otherwise efficient use of force and fraud, and in general to determine and enforce those rules of conduct that give predictability to social relations. This set of conditions is customarily called the institutional framework, and as such has received a great deal of attention.

2. The assumption of rationality itself has been subject to strong and somewhat irrelevant attack, but a critical problem in classical economic

---

* This summary leaves entirely out of account a major aspect of contemporary economic analysis, so-called "macroeconomics," by which is meant the study of national economies as a whole in terms of gross production, national income, and price levels. Since much of this study is explicitly concerned with *changes* in the structure and performance of economic systems, it is discussed in Chapter Five.

theory that has received very little acceptable amendment is the question of ends and motives. The observable facts that ends are not random, wants not unlimited, point to further investigation concerning the character of value systems and the ways in which the individual is induced to comply with the normative order of society.

3. A consideration of a different order concerns the role of groups and combinations in economic activity. Since combinations did not meet the assumptions of a completely competitive order in the older economics, economists have recently begun to study economic principles which take into account the very extensive *organization* of industry and trade. The role of power and authority in the contemporary organization of labor unions and industrial enterprises still tends to be minimized in economic theory and in the dogma of individualism.

By a somewhat artificial distinction, these three ranges of problems may be regarded as most closely related to the body of economic theory, whereas other aspects of the relation of economic systems to societal organization are given subsequent consideration.

Institutional Conditions for Economic Action

Much of the work of sociologists and economists has taken the form of attacks on the abstract principles of the older economics. Some of the attacks, notably those made by the American institutionalists, have simply attempted to dismiss classical theory on the grounds that it was insufficiently descriptive or altogether erroneous. Others have attempted to state a little more clearly the nature of the assumptions made in "liberal" economics and to discover whether such conditions could exist. A very few have proceeded to positive statements of the principles of social order that define or at least limit the sphere of production and trade. As a whole, the studies direct attention to what may be called the "institutional preconditions" for economic organization. (An institution is here regarded as a system of norms, that is, rules of conduct, referring to a major aspect of social life.)

The institutional controls within which any economic system operates must include those governing the division of labor, the disposition of property rights, and the methods of distribution. Stated less austerely, the social order must provide answers to the questions: who does what, who controls what (and whom), and who gets what? The recognition of the cogency of these questions has become increasingly widespread, and considerable research has been devoted to an examination of the influence of variations in these institutions on the economic framework in particular and on the social order in general.

Division of Labor

The importance of the division of labor has long been recognized in economic theory, and indeed formed one of the principal points of interest of Adam Smith. The way in which specialization increases labor productivity is well understood by economists. Division of labor is, however, a much broader problem than is customarily recognized in economic analysis. To set any particular mode of differentiation in its proper perspective, we must know: how the allocation of useful work is accomplished, what determines the type and extent of specialization, how particular labor systems develop, how the specialized workman is fitted into the broader structure of the economy and the society.

Classical labor and wage theory assumed a free and competitive labor market, with few if any restrictions on the ready response of labor supply to market demand. This conceptualization has been subject to two major pressures for modification. On the one hand, the great development of comparative studies of social institutions has served to identify the system of free and mobile labor as one among a rather great variety of labor arrangements.[3] On the other hand, developments in Western societies have served to emphasize variation and change even within modern industrial economies.[4] The two developments in combination lead to a somewhat more adequate understanding of the institutional preconditions for the division of labor.

Labor, to the sociologist, is simply a subconcept of the general concepts of *status* and *role*. An analysis of status determination or role assignment is thus also an analysis of labor arrangements in a broad sense.[5] In a strict sense, labor can be used only where it can be identified by a market test of "useful" activities.

A limited number of studies have investigated specific labor systems and their relation to other conditions, whether natural or social. Nieboer's work on slavery, with materials drawn almost entirely from primitive societies, suggested that forced labor is developed under conditions of open resources and relative ease of subsistence.[6] Marx observed the close relationship between control of rights in valuable things (that is, property) and control over labor, which leads by implication not fully developed by Marx to the hypothetically intimate connection between variations in property arrangements and variations in division of labor.

The minimum division of labor for a social order to function (chiefly the differentiation deriving from the ascribed statuses on the basis of age, sex, and kinship affiliation) is more exactly fixed than is the point of maximum specialization under various conditions. Since modern industrial society has developed along lines of ever-increasing specialization, the societal organization necessary to allow extreme differentiation warrants attention. This was the problem posed and partially resolved by Durkheim, who demonstrated that interdependence alone does not guarantee "social solidarity." Durkheim implied that a normative system in which the individual directly participates is a minimum conditon for extensive occupational specialization.[7]

Specialization raises questions concerning not only the cohesion of the system as a whole, but also the significance of specialized occupational roles for position in the community, life chances, attitudes toward public and private policies and interests, and indeed the whole range of social experience.* Recent studies have provided some new knowledge and understanding of the effects of occupation not only on earnings but on attitudes and ways of life.[8] This leads to the expectation that significant work on the "dimensions" of occupations may go forward in the future. It is probable, for example, that specialization of occupational roles when carried to the extremes exemplified on the assembly line leads to lower productivity than the provision of some variety of tasks. While engineers are constructing machines more like men, social researchers are demonstrating that men are less like machines than had been implicitly assumed in many factory organizations.

In sum, labor and occupation have been shown to be far more complex than was assumed by classical economic theory, and to require extensive sociological investigation now only barely begun.

Property

The control over scarce values, and especially over productive wealth (capital), is an additional institutional arrangement of the highest significance for the ordering of economic production and exchange. Here, as in the case of division of labor, the assumptions made by classical economics were partly wrong in principle (in the sense that they could not exist) and partly and increasingly wrong in fact (in the sense that they no longer exist). The assumptions, usually summarized as "private property," involved at least two principles: that of unlimited rights under unitary control, and that of individual as opposed to group ownership.[9]

The former assumption is intrinsically impossible in view of the necessities of social order that require the reservation of rights by the political

---

* The relation between occupation and social stratification is discussed in Chapter Four.

authority. As a minimum statement, no society could long persist that permitted the widespread use of its scarce values in ways that infringed established rights, or created extensive disorder. In a moderately stable community, private ownership of a gun does not confer rights of unlimited use. Indeed, a householder may be required to cut the ragweed on his lot even if none of his family suffers from hay fever. The factory owner may not produce dangerous or fraudulent goods without controls on his behavior. All of these are infringements on private property.

The assumption of unitary control is only technically fulfilled by the fiction of the corporation as a legal personality, for the modern corporation actually represents extensive division and differentiation of property rights in the assets of company.[10]

Individual ownership exists in all societies, but so does group ownership. Tools, simple weapons, utensils, and articles of apparel are commonly under individual or household control, but land is very commonly under the control of the kinship unit, village, or some other collectivity. In terms of the range of human experience, private control of productive values is no more natural than other arrangements.

The key to the function of property institutions is to be found in the definiton of property as the system of rights of persons or other social units in *scarce* values. It is the scarcity of many social values (including what is ordinarily called wealth) that make necessary regulatory devices for determining who gets what.

Viewed narrowly, property defines the relations of persons to scarce values; viewed more generally it defines relations between persons. A right is meaningless unless there are potential challengers to that right.

To talk of property at all implies therefore an actual or potential power relation between the person holding property rights and the person excluded from their enjoyment. The ideology of private property, particularly as developed in a period of relatively free enterprise, has consistently obscured this point. It has been implicitly recognized at law by successive limitations on the exclusive power of employers to determine the terms of employment and working conditions.

The great power wielded by large concentrations of wealth has been recognized in other ways, of course. Much of the "trust-busting" of the present century has been vainly aimed at squaring traditional doctrine with contemporary economic organization by forcing the "facts" to change to satisfy the assumptions of the law. Yet even this antimonopoly legislation has served to indicate an awareness of the interdependence of modern economic life, and pave the way for even greater extensions of the police power on behalf of workers, investors, and consumers, as well as on behalf of the rights of actual or potential competitors. It is at the present time safe to say that we have so far departed from traditional morality with respect to private enterprise that any large and strategic corporation could not and would not be allowed completely to fail. The precedent is already at hand in the governmental underwriting of banks. There is little doubt that a similarly critical situation in other fields would yield similar or comparable results. Whether these new controls of economic power be called the assertion of human rights as opposed to property rights, or simply tremendous expansion of limitations in the public interest, their significance for property institutions cannot be denied.

The potential complexity of property regulations becomes evident from the very generality of definition one is forced to adopt in order to encompass the range of property phenomena. The complexity arises not only from the large number of valuable "things" which may be the objects of property rights, but from the less generally noted plurality of values attaching to the *same* thing or locus of value. Thus, to take the least abstract case, a given tangible object may be the object of any or all of the following rights: use, transfer, bequest, sale, appropriation of increase or unearned increment, advantageous nonuse, destruction, and so on. This plurality of values, defined and protected by institutional regulation, is obscured by common conceptions of "ownership" of private property. It cannot, however, be neglected if one is to understand the institutional significance of property. Even in a system of private property, some of these potential rights are likely to be controlled or prohibited.

The transferability of property is, however, a key feature of the institutional environment of capitalism. Not only goods and services, but also investment certificates (stocks) and certificates of debt (notes, bonds, mortgages) are bought and sold. Indeed any industrial system, with its characteristic shifts in technology and "product mix," depends upon transferability of control over productive resources. If all capital goods are nominally state-owned, the transfers are effected by administrative decision and bookkeeping entries, but effective and accountable control is still shifted. This illustrates once more the important point that property institutions are complex, and require study in terms of how they operate (their functions), rather than in oversimplified classifications like *public* and *private*.

Exchange

The institutional conditions that define and limit the system of economic exchange and distribution have perhaps received less direct attention than has any other aspect of the relevant institutional framework. The general neglect of distribution in economic theory may partly explain the neglect of the circumstances regulating the distributive system.

By the principles of the older economics, distribution was effected through the system of exchange, beyond which it was unnecessary to go. Under the assumptions of competition and useful specialization, the impersonal market affixed rewards and punishments according to merit. To the extent that the rewards were converted to property rights they were of possible further importance as capital; to the extent that the rewards were converted to consumers' goods they tended to lose all economic significance.

In general, the direct and important factor in distribution was *demand*, which provided part of the dynamic element in the exchange system and together with supply fixed the market price. Now although the demand side of the market equilibrium has been given casual or intensive consideration by economists of various persuasions, the emphasis has been placed on the satisfaction of various wants.

The assumption of distribution according to merit in the productive organization has consistently obscured both the exact nature of the wants to be satisfied, and the significance of familial and other organizational patterns for the allocation of goods among consumers. Although sociologists have understood the function of the family as the consuming unit, they have generally failed to apply this knowledge rigorously in interpreting economic behavior. Yet the application is so clear that it may be taken as established that the behavior of the exchange system is directly affected by the fact that each claim upon the wealth of the society, whether originating in proprietary rights or in claims for services, is likely to represent the claims of a plurality of persons for support. The latter claims rarely rest on merit as economically defined.

By a slight extension of this distributive principle the rationale for some of the modifications imposed on the "free" market becomes understandable: the necessity in an integrated social order of ensuring not only that the market remain genuinely open to those who have recognizable rights to buy or sell but also that values other than the reward for narrowly defined merit be served. These values include the protection of health and the stability of the family. It is the recognition of these values that accounts for governmental definition of minimum standards in wages, hours, working conditions (including safety, workmen's compensation for accidents and industrial diseases, the protection of employed women, and the like), and in rules regarding purity and uniformity of foods and drugs.[11] Other values served by the distributive system are themselves differential in character, being the general principles of stratification and differential valuation prevalent in particular societies. Yet the general conformity of unequal rewards with unequal social position implies no exact relation to merit in the productive system as such.

Once attention is turned to the demand scale as a datum for investigation rather than as a set of conditions that are given, a number of fundamental questions may be raised. Perhaps the most basic theoretical problem is the translation of unlimited and random wants into the sets of ends or goals that lie behind consumer demand. Although the solution to this problem depends upon a more adequate theory of motivation than that commonly used in economics, a minimum and indirect approach is possible by use of economic data.

Familial budget allocations permit appraisal of quantitative and qualitative variations in the hierarchy of wants. The variations in consumption patterns may then be related to occupational and other modes of social distinction.[12] Thus, if families with different income levels are compared cross-sectionally, the budgetary proportions spent for food decrease with higher incomes. The same relationship probably holds for families that have a rising real income through time. It also appears likely that the proportions of income spent for services, as compared with *all* physical goods, increase with higher income levels.

Though the economist in free enterprise economies has generally neglected the differences in consumer preferences, the businessman has not. Thus realistic market analysis takes into account the actual social structure of the community, particularly with respect to varying patterns by which symbols of status are purchased. Consumer surveys are undertaken to appraise volume of demand, effect of price differences, packaging, and various aspects of quality as judged by the actual or potential user.

Business interests not only study consumer choice, but attempt to manipulate it. Experts in advertising must have an implicit sociological orientation in attempting to foster demand for particular products, as well as familiarity with the techniques of deliberate social control, propaganda, and mass communication.

What these homely facts of the economic system illustrate is an elementary principle that should have been evident all along. The system of exchange itself is an eminently social creation, and varies not only according to the modes of production but also according to the social order generally.

Exchange is a necessary counterpart of specialization, however meager that may be. Directly or indirectly it serves not only to allocate goods and services according to some normative principles, but establishes forms of relationships among parties to the transfer.

A peculiarity of a monetary system of exchange is that it minimizes (but does not eliminate) all interpersonal relations except those involved in concluding the bargain. Even in modern economic systems the processes of the market include networks of expectations that in part depend on the character of the trader as well as on what he has in his hands.

In summary, the theoretical foundations for the analysis of the institutional preconditions of economic organization are soundly laid, although the actual principles governing various modes of relationship are unequally developed. The interest of economists in taking into account new conditions may in the future be matched on the part of sociologists seeking the principles of institutional variation and integration.

The Status of Ends and Motives

A question of fundamental importance in the analysis of economic activity is that of the motives that prompt the participation of the actors, or the ends that are to be pursued. It is at this point that the older economics has been subject to attack perhaps even more severe than in the case of the role of institutions.

The assumption of the rational, self-interested individual devoted to the efficient pursuit of unspecified ends, that is, *homo œconomicus*, has created a deal of trouble for economic theory. On the one hand, the theory itself has been internally unstable. In the situation of a plurality of actors, each pursuing his own unlimited ends, any social system would rapidly collapse into "a war of each against all," unless a factually untenable assumption of a "natural identity of interests" was made. The equally untenable alternative was to limit the ends to food, clothing, and shelter. On the other hand, the formula has been subjected to an increasing barrage of evidence pointing to the irrational and nonrational orientation of the human individual to his circumstances and goals. One method of taking this evidence into account is to introduce concepts such as "expectations," which are distinct from ends analytically considered. Expectations include, among other elements, prediction by the entrepreneur of the nonrational conduct of producers or buyers.

Disputes concerning the importance of economic motives or financial incentives abound in the contemporary literature of economics and sociology. The controversies often seem to be marked by an unseemly partisanship, with economists seizing with delight upon each indication that persons respond to monetary inducements, and sociologists showing equal delight when other values seem more important.

At least part of this controversy appears sterile, as it stems from inadequate understanding of the characteristics of human behavior in social systems. Some perspective on the issues may be gained by brief summary statements of the main principles involved.

1. The behavior of the economic man may in fact be approximated within fairly narrow sectors of the social order, and oriented toward ends that by definition in the particular social order are self-interested.

2. The concrete behavior of the social individual, including that of the businessman or laborer in an economic context, is likely to include elements of irrational and nonrational behavior, capable of being understood within the broader framework of the normative order of society.

3. Socially effective motives are in fact primarily of social origin, inculcated through socialization of the young, and usually consistent with the ultimate values held in the society.

4. The approved and market-sanctioned acquisitiveness characteristic of industrial capitalism has in fact had its greatest extension in that economic order, and, in its particular qualities and degree, cannot be regarded as a universal principle of human motivation.

5. The very real economic rationality to be found, for example, in primitive and peasant societies is oriented toward somewhat different goals and is limited by widely varying institutional contexts.

6. It is a serious mistake to equate economic incentives with materialistic goals. Man does not live by bread alone, but in a highly developed market system, money does not buy bread alone. The efficacy of financial incentives is likely to be proportional to the range of individual and group interests and values that can be satisfied through the use of money. With the steady extension of the market to include all sorts of services formerly performed on the basis of kinship obligations or neighborly reciprocity, monetary incentives are of *growing* importance in modern industrial societies.

7. The previous point is not at all negated by increased interest in noneconomic aspects of human behavior and motivation in an economic context (the factory, office, store). The observational and theoretical work prompted by this interest has added greatly to our understanding of the complexity of the individual's relation to the social order. One seemingly elementary but highly important result of this scholarly and practical investigation deserves emphasis. In most social situations, even at the market or workplace, the individual does not *choose* between economic and noneconomic goals or incentives. Many interests may be served concurrently,

and customarily are. In other words, a considerable part of the controversy has been over spurious issues.

The importance of institutional conditions now becomes more evident: they function to integrate the isolated economic act or the particular economic organization into the fabric of the normative order of society. That is, the institutions so "define the situation" that self-interested action also fulfills the expectations of society. This function may be fulfilled with more or less effectiveness; there is no guarantee that the institutional order will be uniformly successful in harmonizing individual and collective interests. Failure to harmonize interests constitutes no disproof of institutional functions, but rather documents the difficulties of achieving integration in a complex society, and especially one where acquisitiveness has been made a dominant goal. Industrial systems depend upon competitive occupational placement, if not upon competitive production and marketing. To the extent that a "culturally fostered discontent" is built into the system, there are necessary costs in the form of possibly disruptive rivalry and contention, and in the form of frustration for the eager but unsuccessful competitor.

Analysis of the institutional framework of economic systems or of the ends and motives of actors in those systems does not disprove economic theory. Rather, it sets the formal analysis of the economic aspects of human behavior within the context of what we know about the structure and operation of societies generally, and of what we know about the relation of individuals to their social world.

Footnotes to Chapter Two

1. Hutchison, Terence Wilmot: A *Review of Economic Doctrines*, Oxford, Clarendon Press, 1953.

2. Parsons, Talcott: *The Structure of Social Action*, New York, McGraw-Hill Book Co., Inc., 1937, pp. 59–60, 63.

3. Moore, Wilbert E.: *Industrialization and Labor: Social Aspects of Economic Development*, Ithaca, N.Y., Cornell University Press, 1951.

4. Moore, Wilbert E.: *Industrial Relations and the Social Order*, rev. ed., New York, The Macmillan Co., 1951, pp. 455–518.

5. Linton, Ralph: *The Study of Man*, New York, D. Appleton-Century Co., 1936, Chap. VII, "Status and Role."

6. Nieboer, H. J.: *Slavery as an Industrial System*, 2nd ed., The Hague, Martinus Nijhoff, 1910, pp. 417–437.

7. Durkheim, Emile: *On the Division of Labor in Society*, trans. by George Simpson, New York, The Macmillan Co., 1933, especially Preface to the Second Edition.

8. Caplow, Theodore: *The Sociology of Work*, Minneapolis, University of Minnesota Press, 1954.

9. Moore, Wilbert E.: "The Emergence of New Property Conceptions in

America," *Journal of Legal and Political Sociology*, 1, Nos. 3–4:34–58 (1943).

10. Berle, Adolf A., Jr., and Gardiner C. Means: *The Modern Corporation and Private Property*, New York, The Macmillan Co., 1933.

11. Moore, Wilbert E.: *Industrial Relations and the Social Order*, pp. 488–493, 606–618.

12. Katona, George: *Psychological Analysis of Economic Behavior*, New York, McGraw-Hill Book Co., Inc., 1951.

chapter three

Economic Theory and Social Organization

The role of authority and power in economic relationships, and the importance of organizations in productive enterprise, provide eminently sociological elements in the interpretation of industrial and commercial affairs. Anglo-American economic theory has until very recently neglected these aspects of economic affairs, and the support by the older legal structure of the abstract conception of a community of independent producers and traders tended to force the hard and uncomfortably negative facts into the mold of abstract theory.

Yet, as in other aspects of economic analysis, the essentially atomistic view of production and exchange has been subject to two types of modification: those directed at the inherent weakness of the theoretical system as such, and those arising from increasing departures from the set of conditions assumed by the older principles.

The classical view of the economic order emphasized a sort of mechanistic interdependence effected by specialization and exchange, but not a system of social relationships. Perhaps the greatest inherent weakness in this view of the economy was the failure to see that in fact private (or any other) property gives a differential access to capital—that, as a result, some producers exchange only labor and not products mixed with labor, and that the system must therefore include authoritarian relationships between the owner or enterpriser and the worker.

Marx and his followers,[1] as well as a number of other German economists, have made the social structure of the productive system a central element in economic theory. Marx thought the power aspects of economic relations would be virtually eliminated by socialist ownership, a view which is not supported by objective analysis. Large-scale organizations with high degrees of specialization of tasks are characteristic of all industrial systems, regardless of proprietary forms. These characteristics are in large part the product of industrial technology, not of the peculiar social institutions of capitalism. Their consequence, in turn, is the authoritative coordination of specialized activities within the business or industrial organization. There are still managers and workers in socialist enterprises, even though they all nominally share in collective ownership.

Despite Marx's confusion of *capitalist* forms of ownership with *industrial* forms of organization, the theory has forced a factual if not a theoretical recognition of the power relationships that are built into the most mechanistically conceived economy.[2]

Combinations and Economic Theory

In legal theory the corporation is treated as a person, with powers to enter contracts, own property, and otherwise act as an individual participant in economic transactions. This conception of corporate personality has consistently obscured the fact that the social invention of the corporation marks a major departure from the ideal of the independent enterpriser. The immense capitalization possible in the corporation means that the single unit is in effect a "combination in restraint of trade." Thus there has gradually grown up a recognition that the corporate form of enterprise forces modification of the older conceptions of risk profits, of ownership and control, and of contractual equality.[3] Moreover, the concept of the *entrepreneur* has had to be modified, since the direction of the enterprise is in fact a *group* responsibility, which gives rise to the problem of determining where, within the single unit, decisions are made.[4]

Trusts, cartels, monopolies, and "price leadership" are represented in recent economic theory as modifications of the traditional conceptions of the independence of producers and the automatic price mechanism of the competitive commodity market.[5] The growth of labor unions has had a somewhat analogous effect upon the competitive labor market.[6]

It is fair to say that with regard to combinations, economic theory has been reluctantly modified to take some account of the crude course of events. Economic theory has been even less dynamic than sociological theory, and has thus said little about long-term changes in economic structure. Marx foresaw the growth of combinations, but erroneously related the trend to the capitalistic drive for profits rather than to the "economies of scale," the advantages of controlling destructive competition, and the administrative efficiencies of bureaucratic organization.

Bureaucratization of Industry and Trade

Perhaps more important than the foregoing from the sociological point of view has been the increasing recognition of the productive or distributive establishment as a complex social organization, amenable to the same general kinds of analysis used with regard to other organizations. Several specialized fields outside of sociology, including industrial management, public administration, and social psychology, have in fact converged upon the complex formal organization as an area for investigation. This has led both to gaps in information and duplication of effort, but a fairly impressive group of principles is emerging.

Bureaucratization implies that economic success for large numbers of people no longer depends upon the impersonal judgment of the market but rather upon the personal judgment of superiors. The entrepreneur's success may depend less upon his correct prognosis of the market than upon his correct prediction of the reaction of workers, whether or not the workers are members of labor unions.

Within the business or industrial organization there is a kind of internal economy, represented by the cost accounting system. An attempt is commonly made to judge the economic success of various units, and to make various judgments partially dependent on that appraisal. There are theoretical possibilities for extension of economic measurement within the organization. For example, what is the cost of information supplied by various staff services, and could that information be obtained more cheaply from independent consulting firms? What is the ratio of overhead (administrative) costs to direct productive costs for units of various sizes, and does this lead to an optimum size of business organization, perhaps variable by type of industry?

The questions just posed imply a kind of economic theory of administrative organization. Such a theory, if gradually developed, will need to depend heavily on conceptions of large organizations that take into account their internal diversification and gradations of authority, lines and channels of communication, and the incentive system that induces people to cooperate in accomplishing the organization's mission.

Stemming partly from the inherently authoritarian structure of productive enterprise, and given greatly added impetus by the tremendous increase in size and specialization of modern firms, there has grown up what might be called a a technology of interpersonal relations for the management of economic activity. There is a tremendous literature, particularly in the United States, on the techniques of management and supervision, methods of selection and promotion, methods of job evaluation, alternative incentives to cooperation, formulas for success in promotion and in selling oneself to superiors, methods of "winning friends and influencing people," and so on.

This development has many facets that cannot be reviewed here in any detail; much of it has taken place without adequate sociological orientation and has thus overlooked the most important aspects of the significant environment in which human activity takes place. Yet it has become increasingly evident that the achievement of cooperation in a competitive and specialized system is one of the principal problems in producing and distributing goods. This fact was long veiled by concentration on the technology of the machine. Recognition of the problem of cooperation was perhaps hindered more than it was helped by an extension of a mechanistic and naively "economic" view toward the management of the human units of production.

Much of the work now identified as industrial sociology has shown how the traditional assumptions about economic incentives and about administrative structures must be modified in view of the social relationships established in the workplace. Some of the studies have exhibited a kind of managerial bias by emphasizing sociological approaches as aiding the technology of personal manipulation. But others have emphasized that interests and perspectives do differ, often even in managerial circles, and that continuous cooperation in production will depend upon serving those interests or compromising differences, rather than on simple financial bribery or little manipulative tricks.

Footnotes to Chapter Three

1. Marx, Karl: *A Contribution to the Critique of Political Economy*, New York, International Library Publishing Co., 1904, especially "Author's Preface." See also Paul M. Sweezy: *The Theory of Capitalist Development*, New York, Oxford University Press, 1942.
2. Boulding, Kenneth E.: *The Organizational Revolution*, New York, Harper & Brothers, 1953.
3. Berle, Adolf, A., Jr., and Gardiner C. Means: *The Modern Corporation and Private Property*, New York, The Macmillan Co., 1933.
4. Gordon, Robert Aaron: *Business Leadership in the Large Corporation*, Washington, The Brookings Institution, 1945.
5. Chamberlin, Edward: *A Theory of Monopolistic Competition*, Cambridge, Harvard University Press, 1933.
6. Dunlop, John T.: *Wage Determination under Trade Unions*, New York, The Macmillan Co., 1944.

chapter four

Economy and Society

|||||||||||||||||||||||||||||||||||||||||||||||||||||||||||||||||||||||||||||||||||||||||||||||||||||||||||||||||||||||||||||||||||||||||||||||||||||||||||||||||||||||||||||||||||

The position of production and trade in the general structure of society raises questions of organizational and institutional interdependence and the functioning of society as a whole. Although the emphasis in the preceding two chapters was on the sociological aspects of the economy viewed as a discrete system, and thus most relevant for economic theory as it has been developed in Anglo-American scholarship, other relationships are also relevant to economic theory. This situation is especially evident in the role of technology as a development largely external to the economic system yet patently of prime importance with respect to materials, methods, and products of economic enterprise. Population growth and composition also affect both the supply of workers and the volume of demand for goods and services.

Other relationships to be investigated are perhaps of less immediate economic significance, but form part of the central structure of sociological theory. They include: the deliberate social controls of the economic order, including economic planning in its various forms, and the effects of these controls not only on the economic organization but upon the entire social structure; the significance of occupation and division of labor for general social status; the relations among economic interest groups and between these groups and other types of organizations; and the reciprocal influences between business and industry on the one hand and the local community on the other.

Technology

The "state of the useful arts" is a matter of central importance to the production of economic goods, yet, as Joseph Spengler and others have pointed out,[1] only part of the determinants of technological development are economic in character. For example, the nature and extent of education, the social support for scientific research, and the types of resistance encountered in various segments of the social structure are all involved. These

24

relationships are examined in greater detail in the following chapter with reference to the interpretation of social change, but are noted here as indicative of functional relationships between economic and noneconomic aspects of social organization.

Population and Labor Force

A quite different range of problems arises with regard to a field long recognized as on the borderline between economics and sociology: the size, characteristics, growth, and distribution of population.

Demography touches economic analysis significantly at two points: the supply of labor, and the demand for goods. These relations are most frequently viewed with respect to the dynamics of population, and there has been a notable tendency to consider population as an empirically independent and even an extrasocial variable.

One standard interpretation, following the teachings of Malthus, has viewed population growth as reducing levels of living, overrunning labor demand, and providing a source of pressures released through war, migration, or economic imperialism. More recent work, however, emphasizes the impossibility of a human population without social organization, and the intimate relation of the latter to variations in the former. Fertility is affected by age at marriage, customs with respect to remarriage of widows, duration of breast-feeding, the physical health of potential parents, and by deliberate controls on conception and pregnancy. Mortality is affected by diet and sanitation, by medical or magical techniques, and to bring the matter full circle, by the rapidity of child-bearing.

The institutional controls of fertility and mortality, which operate somewhat independently of the economic consequences of population movements, are operative in all societies, whether equilibrium depends on high birth and death rates or on a more efficient reproductive balance. Thus the size and rate of change of population constitute not simply noneconomic conditions of significance for economic organization, as was assumed by Malthus. Population size and change are in some respects specifically sociological elements that are economically relevant.

A rapidly growing population provides the basis for growth in economic demand, but does not necessarily add similarly to productive capacity. High birth rates that are eroded by high mortality rates commonly result in substantial wastes of human resources before individuals are old enough to be productive. Even apart from the unfavorable ratio of producers to dependents, implied in rapid growth rates, the sheer burden of supporting the young is likely to have a depressing effect on expenditures for industrial expansion or improvements in technical education. A stable population presents its own economic problems, notably those of possible economic stagnation from the lack of a numerically growing market.

The spread of Western influence, including especially urbanization and industrialization, has added new understanding of the way social structure mediates the relationship between economic systems and population movements. With remarkable uniformity, the impact of the West has been to reduce mortality, without concurrent reduction in fertility. The lag between mortality and fertility reduction was also characteristic of Western experience, but under circumstances of more open spaces and more rapid development of industrial cities than now prevail for the underdeveloped countries of the world.

Appraisal of this historic and contemporary experience reveals that death has a negative value in all societies, but fertility generally has a positive value. Mortality reduction is therefore more acceptable, and involves less direct interference with social organization. Fertility control, which developed historically in the West primarily out of aspirations for economic mobility and improvement, involves a more radical change of social organization and norms. That same process may very well take place in other areas, but the outcome in many is in doubt because mortality can now be reduced faster, and because massive growth may delay or prevent the very economic developments that would theoretically bring about the gradual reduction in fertility.[2]

The recognition of divergent patterns of population growth under different conditions allows the prediction of future population size and composition under varying assumptions, and the analysis of the implications of the projected demographic situations for the economy and society. Although birth rates have been unstable over recent years, death rates have not. It is reasonable to estimate future school populations, size of labor force, or numbers of aged pensioners on the basis of the existing population. The estimation of future births is more hazardous. These other predictions, however, are of profound importance to the economy and society. An accumulating wealth of data and a perfection of techniques may allow fairly rapid expansion of significant generalizations in the future.

Population size and rates of growth and decline affect the demand for economic goods, the degree of flexibility of the productive system, and the impetus for technological change. The age and sex composition of the population affects demand for particular kinds of products and, more importantly, the size, mobility, and quality of the labor force.

Although traditional economic theory, and particularly wage theory, assumed the existence of a large, mobile, and presumably qualified supply of labor, various limitations are apparent on each of these counts. The aging of the labor force in Western societies, together with the prospect for an absolute decline in population of working ages, calls attention to problems of manpower, of obsolescence of skills, and of security for the aged. But the size of the effective labor force is also limited by such essentially noneconomic and nondemographic variables as customs relative to the employment of women and children, the development of a leisure class, and so on.

Similarly, the spatial mobility of the labor force is not completely responsive to slight differentials in economic opportunity, particularly when other features of the social situation are regarded as unfavorable by the potential migrants. Moreover, a dynamic economy requires considerable flexibility in the quality of the labor force. Although the ratio of entrances to departures in the labor force, which is partly a function of population trends, has a bearing on this problem, the institutional and organizational provisions for occupational training and placement are much more important.

In short, the size and composition of the population may be viewed as setting certain limits upon economic organization, but the demographic characteristics themselves are by no means independent of social pressures, and their exact social and economic significance depends upon complex functional relationships.

Occupation and Social Status

Occupational mobility, it has been noted, is relevant to the economy with respect to qualitative and spatial aspects of labor supply. However, this question is more commonly approached by sociologists in terms of the significance of occupation for social stratification.[3] The analysis of occupational position and social status is in fact about as comprehensive as any sociological work in the field of the relations of economy and society. Much of the interest in this field is attributable to the work of Marx and followers of other shades of political opinion and sociological persuasion. A large and on the whole sound literature has developed on the alternative principles of stratification and modes of differential valuation. It seems clear that within a modern industrial society occupation is the most important single (although by no means sole) index of general social position.

The Marxian thesis, that occupation directly determines a class-oriented ideology, has been amply disproved. It especially neglects the dynamic element of socialization, which is, however, class-differentiated and thus certainly provides an indirect basis for occupational determination of ideology. The fact that children are born into families with unequal incomes and that their training and opportunities are differentiated according to social strata also serves to explain in part the often-demonstrated departures in practice from the open-class ideology of equal opportunity and free mobility. The comparative literature in this field is reasonably abundant, but is inadequately grounded in theory and therefore often provides no answers to questions concerning occupational specialization and the differential social valuation of occupational roles. It may, however, be maintained that occupation is never irrelevant for social status, although the dynamic relationship appears to be reversed under a caste situation. Indeed, it appears, and not surprisingly, that the independent importance of occupation is in direct ratio to the emphasis upon economic production in the social order.

The economic function of occupational mobility in a modern industrial system is clearly that of maintaining flexibility in labor supply in view of changes in technology and "product mix." To fulfill this function it is not necessary that all workers, or even all workers of a given category, be equally sensitive to changing demand and differences in opportunity. A mobile minority will ordinarily preserve the necessary flexibility of supply.

Flexibility of labor supply involves several different types of mobility. Theoretically the barriers to movement are least when it involves solely change of employers at the same occupation (whether or not in the same industry) in the same community. Geographical movement obviously entails greater economic costs and social penalties. Occupational movement that entails employment at a higher level of skill requires the acquisition of the appropriate skill either through experience or formal training. Because of the length-of-training element, there are inherent frictions to free mobility in any occupational system.

The sociological function of mobility is analogous with this situation in some respects, but has other dimensions. Occupational mobility that represents genuine change of status serves to prevent rigidification of a stratification system that is officially "open," and belief in such opportunities serves to confirm the stability of the normative system. Again, it is not necessary for everyone to be equally mobile for these functions to be fulfilled. However, individual failure to achieve or reasonably approximate aspirations for improvement in economic and social position necessarily produces some frustration and sources of tension.

The amount of occupational mobility is clearly partly a function of how finely occupations are distinguished and classified. The analysis of mobility in terms of a few broad occupational categories may conceal a great deal of movement that is both economically and sociologically significant. A man may, for instance, move from a junior executive position in a corporation to a top-level job, with very considerable change in power, organizational status, and income. He will not be counted as mobile if the standard class (as used by the U. S. Census, as well as many nongovernmental researchers) "managers, proprietors, and officials" is employed in measuring mobility. It must also be recognized that movement between occupations that require long periods of training is understandably rare, but that these occupations (for example, the learned professions) exhibit wide internal differences in income and reputation. An individual may thus move up in his profession without the moves appearing in standard measures of occupational mobility.

Occupational as other types of status mobility occurs not only in single careers, but between generations. Essentially the same economic and social functions are served by intergenerational as by intragenerational mobility. Putting the question in generational terms adds long-term considerations to current "functions," regardless of trend.

This last point may be argued negatively for its economic aspects, positively for its sociological significance. A rigid inheritance of occupation would not only introduce extensive inflexibilities in occupational placement and limitations on choice and competition, but would also require exact demographic reproduction according to the openings to be filled. More positively, intergenerational mobility serves to confirm the approximation to the ideal of equality of opportunity and to reduce the frustration of career failure by projection of parental aspirations to the children. This leads parents to make sacrifices in order to secure education for their children. Children are taught to be competitive, to be dissatisfied with their parents' achievements, and to be anxious for success. No doubt considerable impetus to innovation and "progress" comes from this basic source.

Finally, not all significant mobility, even of an income-and-occupation sort, takes place within the individual's active career. The channels of movement include notably formal education, so that considerable differences in "life chances" are already settled by the time individuals enter the labor market.[4] This circumstance has a major bearing on appraising temporal trends in the amount of social mobility.

Social Controls of the Economic Order

Some aspects of the relations between economy and society comprise those previously discussed as of central importance to an understanding of the internal operation of the economic system. Thus, the regulatory devices that are normally called the "social controls of industry" may be properly regarded as an elaboration of the institutional conditions bearing on economic activity. The significance of these controls in sociological theory, however, is not simply that they are conditions for economic action. They not only *limit* but also in the broadest sense *define* economic action.

The "conditions" from the point of view of economic theory are actually central structural elements in the cohesiveness of society. For in the process of limiting economic action they determine the ends that the economy should serve, and the additional values with which it should be consistent.

A rough classification of the controls on the economy follows:[5]

1. *Protection of "economic opportunity."* Preservation of access to the market, control of monopolies and other combinations, enforcing public responsibility on large-scale corporations.

2. *Protection of investors.* Regulation of equity stock issuance and sales, requirement of reports to stockholders and provision for voting for corporate officers.

3. *Protection of the consumer.* Requirements of grade-labeling, prevention of adulterated, harmful, or fraudulent foods and drugs.

4. *Protection of employment standards.* Provisions for minimum wages and maximum hours. Control of the labor of women, children, or other "substandard" workers.

5. *Reduction of risks.* Enforcement of safety regulations, provision of various forms of insurance against the hazards of unemployment, illness, old-age support.

The ends and values involved in such regulation of the economy clearly do not relate solely to its efficient, competitive operation, or even to insuring equity in economic matters. Health, preservation of the family, and rising levels of general education are among the other values served by the deliberate "interference" in the conduct of manufacturing and trade.

The modern deliberate controls of industry simply provide new conditions for the economist, and these conditions may either be taken into account and new principles formulated for those circumstances, or they may be neglected at the expense of increasing "unreality" (that is, abstractness) of existing theory.

For the sociologist the controls raise a series of problems barely touched upon in contemporary theory. For example, to what extent is it possible to plan a society? What organizational structure is most effectively designed to achieve a given set of values with the least possible sacrifice?

Economic Interest Groups

The facts of modern organization and combination in industrial enterprises and commercial establishments, and among occupational and professional groups, leads to still another field for sociological inquiry: the principles governing the relations of groups within the economic order. In general, the sociologists may perhaps safely neglect the relations between industrial enterprises so long as these are primarily market phenomena, although even here the problems of new controls for the benefit of unrepresented but legitimate interests require the type of functional analysis increasingly prevalent in sociological research.

The relations between managers and laborers, particularly in the development of collective bargaining, are even less amenable to analysis in terms of labor supply and demand. It is evident that new principles of social organization are being worked out, mostly on a sheerly empirical basis, but offering opportunities for both application and expansion of sociological theory. Thus, economists and sociologists alike have observed the development of a kind of industrial jurisprudence or common law growing out of collective bargaining, contract interpretations, and arbitration. This common law is largely outside the framework of the formal statutes and decisions, but obviously ultimately accountable to the fundamental legal principles.

Analysis of the collective relations between managements and unions has generally taken the form of typologies—for example, the range from *conflict* to *cooperation*, or the distinction between *pattern-setting* and *pattern-following*. Temporal trends have received less attention, partly because of the rapidity of short-term changes in law and practice. It does appear, however, that several continuing trends may be predicted: (a) broadening the scope of bargaining in the sense of kinds of issues brought to discussion; (b) an expansion in the number and size of units included in single negotiations—for example, between national unions (or coalitions of such unions) and employers' associations; and (c) the mutual influence on the internal structure of corporations and unions—a parallel bureaucratization —through bargaining and grievance procedures.

The elaborate development of economic interest groups raises many other questions not treated here, including that of the distribution of power among these groups and between any particular power group and the state. The existence and multiplicity of such groups indicate not only the complexity of the associational character of modern society, but also the intricacy of connections among economic, political, and social aspects of life where they superficially seem to be separate. The National Association of Manufacturers is explicitly dedicated to the interests of industrial corporations, and seeks to influence public opinion and legislation as part of its program. The American Medical Association is explicitly dedicated to the improvement of medical education and practice, but it also spends a major portion of its resources trying to influence public opinion and legislation on behalf of the financial rather than professional interests of physicians.

Business and the Local Community

Some of the foregoing problems are most pointedly illustrated in the local community, where the interdependence of economic organization and communal affairs is a daily observable phenomenon. Ecological studies have thrown considerable light upon the economic factors in community location and internal structure, as well as on the process of community growth and structural change. These studies illustrate the way changes in land use and transportation affect the geography of a city as well as its social organization.

The industrial plant and the local community are in a situation of mutual dependence. In terms of power, the balance may be tipped in either direction. Thus industrial communities range from small company towns under the fairly extensive control of the business firm to the diversified industrial city which has a minimum of dependence on any one company. Even in the larger community, however, research studies indicate that business leaders occupy positions of power in the community outside their formal corporate positions.[6]

Political authorities or business leaders in a community may offer various inducements to companies planning to move or expand their plants. But local interests may also seek to "bleed" established plants in terms of tax rates, or to control industrial processes in terms of noise abatement, disposal of wastes, or development of new power sources. Industrial managers may choose a new plant location partly because workers are unlikely to join unions. They may subsequently find their workers unionized and also organized politically in order to have a voice in community affairs.

Over recent years American manufacturing corporations have paid increasing attention to the "community responsibilities of management." Critics of corporate policy point out that "responsibilities" *may* be another way of expressing "influence" or even "domination." In general, some separation of economic and political organization and power seems as essential to preservation of democratic forms of government as does the separation of church and state.

Footnotes to Chapter Four

1. Spengler, Joseph J.: "Sociological Presuppositions in Economic Theory," *Southern Economic Journal*, 7, No. 2:131–157 (1940).

2. Davis, Kingsley: "The World Demographic Transition," *Annals of the American Academy of Political and Social Science*, 237:1–11 (1945).

3. Bendix, Reinhard, and Seymour Martin Lipset, eds.: *Class, Status and Power: A Reader in Social Stratification*, Glencoe, Ill., The Free Press, 1953, pp. 388–442.

4. West, Patricia Salter: "Social Mobility among College Graduates," in *ibid.*, pp. 465–480.

5. Moore, Wilbert E.: *Industrial Relations and the Social Order*, rev. ed., New York, The Macmillan Co., 1951, pp. 606–618.

6. Hunter, Floyd: *Community Power Structure: A Study of Decision Makers*, Chapel Hill, University of North Carolina Press, 1953.

chapter five

The Interpretation of Social Change

A great many scholars, impressed by the extreme rapidity of social change, have sought explanations in the dynamic relations between economy and society. The most widely held views, unsupported either by fact or logic, attribute primary causal significance to economic factors in social change. All may be called forms of "economic determinism." The varying emphases may be conveniently reduced to four: the primacy of economic (roughly, hedonistic) motives, the inherent dynamics of economic organization and institutions, the independent expansion of industrial technology, and the innovating role of the entrepreneur, which, in one view of economic change, constitutes the essential dynamic element in modern industrial capitalism.

There are two other aspects of socio-economic change. One is the far-reaching and yet little noted significance of changing occupational structures in modern industrial societies. The other is the process of industrialization itself. The historic developments in Western societies are now being repeated, in some form or degree, throughout the world. The breadth of evidence through time and place allows an almost experimental approach to uniform and variable elements in the process of economic change.

Economic Determinism

Of the four principal types of economic determinism, the primacy of materialistic motives is least often supported as an explicit cause, but it is implicitly assumed in a vast range of economic literature. Knowledge of extensive cultural variability of values and motives has sufficed to prevent most sociologists from subscribing to the view.

The thesis that the character of the economic organization shapes the main contours of the social order, and provides the initial impetus to societal changes, has received more elaborate development. Perhaps the clearest exposition is still that of Marx and his interpreters. According to Marx, the character of society is fundamentally determined by the "economic factor," including resources, technology, and productive organization.

The difficulty with this position in general is that the economic factor is poorly identified and indeed upon close examination is found to include elements perfectly capable of variation quite independently of productive or market organization. Such, for example, is the case with property. If the economic factor is defined so as to include most of the institutional features of society, then to attribute primary causal significance to it in the interpretation of social change loses all precision. At the extreme, this becomes a theory that "everything causes everything," which is not very helpful.

An economic interpretation which has gained wide currency in sociology views social change in terms of resistance and adaptations to expanding technology, the latter regarded as inherently accumulative or dynamic. Veblen's maintenance of this position was largely confined to economic developments in recent times, and did not entirely neglect the independent significance of nontechnological values—which Veblen, however, is inclined to lump under the heading of "vested interests."[1] More recent adaptations of the position, particularly as exemplified in the "culture lag" hypothesis, have been less restrained in the claims made, and have done considerably more violence to fact and logic.

Perhaps the greatest difficulty in the assessment of the accuracy of the various forms of "economic interpretations" is the definition and identification of the variables. As previously noted, few sociologists have subscribed to the patently erroneous view that all human behavior may be reduced to the struggle for existence, the "acquisitive instinct," or the satisfaction of economic wants expressed in mainly physiological terms. It is rather in the conditions, forms, and organization of productive enterprise that most adherents to the doctrine of economic primacy find their prime mover. Marx and his followers, for example, have emphasized the effect of technology and "relationships of production" in providing the dynamic factors that lead to the gradual or sudden transition from one productive system to another. Two difficulties are encountered in this interpretation:

1. The economic factor so defined includes a number of distinct elements, at least some of which are independently variable. It thus becomes difficult to assess precisely what dynamic role is to be assigned to each of the elements. The fact of independent variability has an even further significance, for some of the elements are economically relevant, but are far from being determined by other elements. Thus, property arrangements may be modified to give more or less power to an employer, or profits taxed away to provide unemployment relief or to finance an international war. The exploitative power of the owner of capital may be regulated by law, and the terms of the wage contract limited by legislation designed to protect the

health of children. These are changes in the conditions and relationships of production; but the dynamic lies outside the economic organization, in norms and institutions, and not the other way around.

Actually, of course, a functional relationship holds, and its interpretation may be conveniently approached by primary attention to changes in the productive organization. The difficulty lies in claiming that this matter of convenience is something more—that it represents the true basis of societal organization. It is perhaps equally convenient to examine the functional relationships from any other starting point.

2. Above all, however, it is necessary to examine the character of the conditions not included as elements in the economic factor but which are in fact conditions necessary for the supposed course of economic development actually to take place. Notable in this respect is the constancy of ends. The explicit denial by various economic determinists that any assumption is made concerning the primacy of economic motives, and the partially accurate insistence that the behavior of specific individuals is rather a function of their position in the system, do not eliminate the relevance of ends.

One form of productive enterprise will lead to a more efficient or more highly organized form only so long as and to the extent that the value system remains reasonably favorable to the change. When conflicts of interests, economic and otherwise, arise, as they inevitably must in a dynamic situation, the victory of certain interests depends upon the whole normative and structural situation. There is no *a priori* reason for supposing that economic interests will prevail. Neither is there an *a priori* reason for supposing that the economic structure is any more immanently dynamic than any other.

The Role of Technology

A current and very popular mode of interpretation of social change places primary or exclusive emphasis on an inherently expanding technology. Its popularity seems to be a function of its simplicity, and partly a fortuitous result of its being superficially correct for some of the data arrayed under its aegis. In its crudest form this interpretation attempts to draw a distinction between accumulative material culture (machines, tools, artifacts), and nonmaterial or adaptive culture (ideas, knowledge, values).[2] This view makes the initial error of failing to see that culture objects are only part of the culture in so far as they embody ideas and values, and that the same objects may have substantially different functional significance in other cultural contexts. The attention to the material culture has left the impression that machines are self-inventing, self-perpetuating, and self-expanding, and that nonmaterial culture tends to lag behind the existing pile of objects.

A more tenable formulation makes of technology (which is a system of ideas, principles, and interests) a segment of culture more subject to change than other aspects of culture, and therefore possibly of causal significance in social change. Under certain conditions this proposition is likely to be correct, precisely because of the *instrumental* character of technology. That is, the elaboration of techniques for the achievement of some societal values is likely to require modification of other practices and possibly of beliefs. Thus, changes in the design and performance of automobiles have certainly "caused" modification of American recreational customs, and have been relevant to changes in courtship ideals and practices. Likewise, the increased mechanization of industry has increased the competitive advantage of large industries and "caused" considerable industrial transformations.

The error of attributing sole or primary causal importance to an expanding technology has consisted in the neglect of the important qualification, "under certain conditions." These conditions may be briefly stated.

For technological change to be *primary* the end or goal of technological progress must be assumed, and must remain constant. A change of ends makes previous technology wasteful, and creates a temporary lag in the development of a new technology. Thus a nation at war finds its peacetime industrial technology oriented toward ends that are no longer primary (such as refrigerators and automobiles) and its wartime production limited by an inadequate technology. In this case it is obviously the goal that is of causal significance in the change, and not the technology.

The doctrine of technological primacy has had some validity in the interpretation of industrial transformation, precisely because the goal of economic productivity has been more or less correctly assumed, and has remained reasonably constant. Other scientific principles could be applied to other practical (that is, socially approved) ends, and to a considerable degree have been in such fields as medicine, public health, and even propaganda and social control.

As a universally valid principle the technological interpretation of social change is forced to find some source of the ends to be achieved. Thus, there is a marked tendency for this view to become a watered-down version of the doctrine of economic causation, and fall heir to the difficulties of that doctrine as well.

Among the proponents of the primacy of technological change there is evident an unmistakable tone of moral disapproval directed against the lags —that is, resistances to structural and normative adaptations occasioned by innovation. Were there no such counterbalancing of technical changes, the social structure would collapse, or rather, would not have existed in the first place.

Inventions, then, do have social results; they also have social causes, and their acceptance or rejection depends upon the social framework. Some of the results are likely to be unanticipated. If those unanticipated results are changes that the existing structure is poorly designed to accept or incorporate they will result in culture lag.

But culture lag is certainly not the predestined result of the slowness of adaptive culture in catching up with the inevitably changing material culture; the lag is in fact capable of purposive solution. It is possible to adjust to the machine (thus preserving the dominance of the original goal, but modifying others), or it is possible to change, modify, regulate, or abandon the machine in view of other values. Even in the modern industrial world the dictum that "You cannot fight social (that is, technological) trends" is discounted by the fact that inventions are customarily controlled when their results would be contrary to business interests.

Entrepreneurship

In classical economic doctrine, the factors of production were land, labor, and capital. Their use in the productive process yielded three forms of income: rent, wages, and interest, respectively. Subsequent modifications of economic analysis often added a fourth productive factor: the entrepreneur. As originally conceived the entrepreneur was a manager (and thus, a type of laborer) but also a risk-taker. The risk-taking function yielded a fourth type of income, profits.

This conception of the economic system was not, strictly speaking, static as long as the factors of production were not entirely used, and used in their most favorable proportions. But beyond that point, the conceptual scheme provided for little change in economic structure.

As an essentially new interpretation of economic history, the late Joseph A. Schumpeter offered a different conception of the entrepreneur.[3] This approach made of the entrepreneur an *innovator*: whether of products, productive techniques, or organizational arrangements.

This reinterpretation raised questions of sociological interest not previously noted in economic history, such as the social conditions for the development and success of economic innovators. In Schumpeter's view, a view which was partially developed on the basis of the work of Marx and Weber, early capitalist development depended upon innovators who broke loose from conventional processes and ideas of economic propriety.

Schumpeter does suggest, however, that a social order already undermined was essential to the success of entrepreneurs.

This innovating function of the entrepreneur is not really antithetical to the earlier concept of risk-taking. It puts the latter in a dynamic context. Schumpeter adds that with the organization of the modern corporation, both entrepreneurial functions have become "obsolescent." In the modern large corporation the entrepreneur is a possibly useful fiction of economic analysis. Decisions of all sorts, including decisions on new products and processes, are the consequences of interdependent group action, with the pooling and compromising of competences and personal views and influences.

The entrepreneurial interpretation of economic change leads, however, to an important aspect of modern economic organization—*the organization and institutionalization of change*. People are employed, capital invested, and organizational resources are committed to constant change in organization, process, and product. Research is a major component of modern industrial activity, and is by no means confined to research departments.

This commitment to deliberate change, which provides some of the seeming support for types of technological determinism, is not limited to business and industry. Schools and universities, legislatures, and many governmental agencies are committed to advancing knowledge, improving current practice, and rectifying abuses.

It is possible to argue, on somewhat shaky evidence, that the economic innovator has been more highly rewarded than others. On still shakier evidence, it might even be alleged that entrepreneurship in this sense has set the pace for social change generally. The solid fact is that modern industrial societies not only change rapidly, but in large measure deliberately.

Changing Occupational Structure

Technological change in production, whether of products or processes, has important consequences for the demand for skills in the labor force. Three such consequences can be distinguished: the obsolescence of skills, the dilution of skills, and the demand for new skills.

Skills are made obsolescent by the declining demand for particular products and by mechanization of operations. Dilution of skills is mainly the consequence of specialization of tasks, often in conformity with mechanical processes. This is what is usually meant by *division* of labor, and what is usually commented on adversely with reference to the subservience of labor to the machine.

A correlative development is less often noted as an aspect of changing technology and organization—the demand for new skills, including the design of processes, the coordination of specialized activities, and the supply of information.

The general significance of these concurrent changes in occupational role is rather markedly different from that painted by ardent critics of capitalism and industrialism. The processes of mechanization and large-scale organization have not produced a growing mass of unskilled and routinized workers, supervised by a handful of bosses.

On the contrary, the major changes through time have been the steady reduction of the proportion of unskilled workers, and the growing proportions of semiskilled and skilled workers, and particularly of clerical, technical, managerial, and professional workers. The handicraft worker is often displaced by mechanization, it is true. But at later stages, the servant of the machine is often displaced by the machine designer, the machine builder, and the machine master.

The changing occupational structure of industrial societies may be seen within the business enterprise, and in the economy as a whole. Within the enterprise, the most notable trends are the growing number of distinct occupations, a specialization made possible by the large scale of operations, and the growing proportion of clerical, administrative, and staff positions relative to production workers. In the larger scene the same shifts are manifest. Even if all employees of manufacturing corporations are viewed as "engaged in manufacturing," which is not true in an occupational sense, this sector of the labor force has diminished rather than grown in the United States over recent decades. Services of all sorts, including finance, transportation, and distribution, but also including repairs, professional practice, and entertainment, represent growing proportions of total occupations and of national income.

These trends in occupational structure have rather far-reaching but largely unnoticed implications for theories of long-term economic change. They suggest, for example, that the Marxian theory of increasing "polarization" of the economically active population into "capitalists" and the "proletariat" is radically false. Indeed, the division between bosses and workers appears sharpest at very early stages of industrialization (when Marx observed and speculated).[4] By extension, the steady diversification of occupations, and the tendency of distinct occupational interests to take priority over collective loyalties to management or labor, undermine the internal solidarity of these categories.

Changes in occupational structure also throw light on some disputed issues with respect to trends in occupational mobility and, in this sense, economic opportunity. A common, and quite factually unsupported, doctrine of our time is that mobility has slowed up and classes have become more rigid since the last century. Had the structure not changed, there is some evidence that upward mobility within single *occupational* careers would have declined, but not necessarily within single lifetimes in view of the growing importance of education as a ladder, and its expanding availability. Advanced education not only allows an individual to start at a higher position (and thus to have been mobile before he enters an occupation) but also improves his chances of mobility later. But the argument that mobility is declining is tendentious indeed when account is taken of the tremendous expansion of jobs to be filled at least in middle positions (as measured by income or prestige).

Industrialization and Economic Growth

One of the most sweeping movements of modern times is the spread of the industrial system and its products to all parts of the world. In many areas the penetration has been recent and small, but it is significant for its present impact on traditional social structures as well as for its implications for the future.

The industrialization process relates to a general theory of social change in at least three ways indicated by the following questions: (1) Are there relatively standard sequences of changes in the structure of economies through industrial development, valid through time and space? (2) Are there predictable consequences for traditional social structures with the advent and development of industrial modes of production? (3) Are there principles of social change that will account for the form and rate of industrialization in relatively underdeveloped areas?

That these questions are rarely asked and currently scarcely answerable is further evidence of the neglect of theories of long-term change in both economics and sociology.

Available evidence provides some partial answers, and affords the opportunity for some speculations.

To the question about standard sequences, a tentative yes can be hazarded. From the history of Western industrial countries, it appears that the most rapid *rate* of economic growth may have moved through the following stages:[5]

1. Food production and agriculture generally
2. Physical manufacture
   a. Physical capital (transportation, power, plant, machines)

    b. Consumer nondurables
    c. Consumer durables
  3. "Industrialization" of agriculture
  4. Technical skills and services
    a. Experts on the nonhuman environment
    b. Experts on human motivation and organization

It should be noted that in a highly industrialized system all of these aspects of production are to some extent concurrent. The hypothesis advanced here relates simply to priorities in the allocation of resources and their changes through time. It is also probable that late-comers to the industrialization process (the underdeveloped countries) will import plant and equipment, and some technical skills, and will start manufacturing with consumer nondurables. The latter tend to be labor-intensive (and labor is generally in abundant numerical supply) rather than capital-intensive (and capital is clearly in short supply).

To the question of the impact of industry on the structure of society, at least partial answers are available. Industrialization involves urbanization in some degree, and is uniformly destructive of extended kinship systems (where binding mutual obligations prevail among many relatives of various degrees), and traditional modes of social stratification. In one way or another, all of these consequences are linked to the industrialization process by the *mobility* required by the latter.

To account for the marked success of industry in penetrating primitive and agrarian societies, and at the same time to account for the highly unequal rates of economic change, requires an extensive analysis that has largely not been undertaken. Why are France and Italy so little industrialized as compared with England and Germany, despite an earlier start? Why did Japan, with limited resources and rigid stratification, industrialize and China, with greater resources and a relatively "open" class system, not do so? It is obvious, but not precisely helpful, that values and institutional arrangements differ, as do resources, climate, population, and other elements relevant to production. A truly general theory of economic growth cannot be formulated until the complexity and diversity of social experience are better known and better understood.

Footnotes to Chapter Five

1. Veblen, Thorstein: *The Vested Interests and the State of the Industrial Arts*, New York, B. W. Huebsch, 1919; also, Veblen: *The Engineers and the Price System*, New York, B. W. Huebsch, 1921.
2. Ogburn, William F.: *Social Change*, New York, Viking Press, 1936.

3. Schumpeter, Joseph A.: *Capitalism, Socialism, and Democracy*, 3rd ed., New York, Harper & Brothers, 1950.

4. Moore, Wilbert E.: "Occupational Structure and Industrial Conflict," in Robert Dubin, Arthur Kornhauser, and Arthur Ross, eds.: *Industrial Conflict*, New York, McGraw-Hill Book Co., Inc., 1954. See also Moore: *Industrialization and Labor*, Ithaca, Cornell University Press, 1951.

5. This "stage theory of economic growth" represents a speculative extension of data and ideas presented by Simon Kuznets in a paper, as yet unpublished, "Toward a Theory of Economic Growth," prepared for the Columbia University Bicentennial Conference on "National Policy for Economic Welfare at Home and Abroad," May, 1954.

chapter six

Livelihood and Life

Developments during the present century in the general field reviewed here appear on the whole to be auspicious for the future. Despite a seeming reluctance of many sociologists, particularly in the United States, to devote attention to the scientific problems at hand, substantial strides have been taken. It should be noted, however, that there is no good reason for maintaining that all aspects of economic behavior not included in classical economics is sociological by default.

Economic principles may be formulated under numerous conditions besides those of a "liberal" economic order. It is noteworthy that comparative economics has been little developed, and that a considerable area for economic research remains open both in modern Western societies and in other types of social orders.

The seeming autonomy of the economic system in Western societies may in part account for attempts to construct a "pure" economics that is at the same time concretely descriptive of business affairs. However, that autonomy is illusory, as this study has been at pains to point out, and there is no theoretical reason for failing to apply scientific analysis to economic elements in any society where a monetary-market system prevails.

Even were such an expansion in economic theory to take place, however, large questions for sociological inquiry would remain. The development of new economic principles under changing social conditions and the extensive sociological analysis of those conditions combine to document what should have been evident all along, as emanating from the logic of science: namely, that economic laws like any others are universal only in abstraction and will operate only within the conditions upon which they are based. Only much more comparative investigation will reveal how many of the relevant conditions are empirically universal, and why.

With respect to the values and regulatory principles that provide the social setting for economic behavior, sociological development has been substantial. Beyond the establishment of the general importance of these struc-

44

tural elements in society, there has been achieved an approximate identification of the necessary limits to variability in some economic relations and behavior: the limits to economic rationality as a scheme for social behavior, the limits of private property, and the limits of occupational specialization. Short of these limits, knowledge is understandably most extensive concerning Western industrial society. Extensive research has indicated the relations between income and occupation on the one hand and general social position on the other. However, lack of familiarity with the results, or the ease of maintaining less adequate conceptions (such as the common identification of upper, middle, and lower classes), stand in the way of advanced research.

Future research needs to be turned particularly to much more extensive comparative and functional analysis of institutions, with particular regard to specific relationships in institutional and organizational forms. This applies even to modern Western society. To what extent can "free institutions" be incorporated within a social order exercising extensive control over production and distribution? Does a system of collective bargaining in labor relations necessarily lead to an increasing emphasis on stability of status, and on organized class relations? Answers to these questions may have a bearing on public policy as well as on the general body of scientific theory.

The present century has witnessed a slow but steady reaffirmation of the distinctly human data of social life, especially the categorically demonstrable fact that ends and ideas make a difference. With respect to economic behavior, less emphasis has been placed on the subjective orientation of the actor (which is generally *assumed* in economic theory) than upon the character of the ends and their approximate consistency with the normative expectations of society.

The relative effectiveness of various normative systems in securing the production of economic goods and services cannot yet be assessed. Moreover, the significance of the increasing use of money as a universal means is perhaps not fully understood. For example, to what extent does "pecuniary emulation" tend to break down occupational ethics that have traditionally emphasized disinterested behavior, as in medicine?

The principles of bureaucratic organization, applicable to industrial enterprises, are fairly certain. Preliminary research has undertaken the study of the informal organization that may be confidently expected in highly specialized structures. Yet much of the work of specialists in industrial management is limited to the discovery, but not the analysis, of the human factor as a residual category. The field remains open for the development of principles that will determine the limits to segmentation of roles in formal structures, and provide systematic formulation of the social conditions for the operation of specialized organizations.

Finally, there is necessary an entire restatement of the theory of social change and of the methodological problems in the analysis of social change. With reference to the role of economic organization and industrially oriented technology, much time and labor have been wasted in demonstrating the obvious and completely misinterpreting its significance. This is especially evident in the culture-lag hypothesis. Yet little is actually known of the long-term structural changes in industrial economies or the necessary conditions for industrialization in societies outside the main lines of Western economic development.

There is, of course, no requirement within the scientific ethic that research should be practical in the sense of being immediately applicable for the achievement of ends other than the advance of knowledge. However, it is at least politic for a body of scientists to attempt to provide facts relevant to the determination of public policy. Whatever may be said for the merit of the field under review with respect to the advancement of science, the growing importance of economic problems in the modern world suggests that sociologists may find it appropriate to devote renewed attention to the social behavior of economic man.

Selected Readings

||||||||||||||||||||||||||||||||||||||||||||||||||||||||||||||||||||||||||||||||||||||||||||||||||||||||||||||||||||||||||||||||||||||||||||||||||||||||||||||||||||||||||||||||

BENDIX, REINHARD, and SEYMOUR MARTIN LIPSET: *Class, Status and Power: A Reader in Social Stratification*, Glencoe, Ill., The Free Press, 1953.
  Contains selections from most of the classic theories of social stratification, together with a wealth of descriptive materials on economic and social inequality.

BOULDING, KENNETH E.: *The Organizational Revolution: A Study in the Ethics of Economic Organization*, New York, Harper & Brothers, 1953.
  The author, an outstanding economist, appraises the significance of large corporate enterprise, not only for economic theory but also for social policy.

CAPLOW, THEODORE: *The Sociology of Work*, Minneapolis, University of Minnesota Press, 1954.
  A comprehensive and highly readable sociological approach to occupation, division of labor, labor markets, and the impact of technology on working conditions.

DRUCKER, PETER F.: *The New Society: The Anatomy of Industrial Order*, New York, Harper & Brothers, 1950.
  A popular interpretation of the significance of the corporate character of business enterprise. The theories advanced are subject to argument, but the author recognizes social changes commonly neglected.

FIRTH, RAYMOND: *Primitive Polynesian Economy*, London, George Routledge and Sons, 1939.
  One of several books by the author, who recognizes the difficulties of singling out "economic" behavior in a primitive society, and shows the intricate connections between productive activities and all others.

HUTCHISON, TERENCE WILMOT: *A Review of Economic Doctrines, 1870–1929*, Oxford, Clarendon Press, 1953.
  An able summary of recent economic theory, which unlike many "histories of doctrines," takes into account modern developments.

JAFFE, A. J., and CHARLES D. STEWART: *Manpower Resources and Utilization: Principles of Working Force Analysis*, New York, John Wiley & Sons, Inc., 1951.
  Contains much statistical and descriptive material on changes in occupational structure, set within a framework of economic, demographic, and sociological analysis.

KUZNETS, SIMON: *Economic Change: Selected Essays in Business Cycles, National Income, and Economic Growth*, New York, W. W. Norton & Company, Inc., 1953.

A series of technical papers, which are nevertheless lucidly written, by a leading representative of macroeconomics.

MERTON, ROBERT K., and Others, eds.: *Reader in Bureaucracy*, Glencoe, Ill., The Free Press, 1952.

Essays on complex administrative organizations in their various aspects. Some of the papers apply specifically to industrial bureaucracies, and many others discuss features common to all administrative structures.

MILLER, DELBERT C., and WILLIAM H. FORM: *Industrial Sociology: An Introduction to the Sociology of Work Relations*, New York, Harper & Brothers, 1951.

Traces the scholarly roots of industrial sociology. This book is especially rich in descriptive materials on work relations, and on the social adjustment of the worker at various standard stages of a career.

MOORE, WILBERT E.: *Industrial Relations and the Social Order*, rev. ed., New York, The Macmillan Company, 1951.

A revision of the first general book on industrial sociology, which deals both with the social organization of the industrial enterprise and with the various relations between industry and society.

MOORE, WILBERT E.: *Industrialization and Labor: Social Aspects of Economic Development*, Ithaca, Cornell University Press, 1951.

A systematic review of evidence on attitudes toward industrial work in newly developing countries, together with a critique of labor theory in economics.

SCHUMPETER, JOSEPH A.: *Capitalism, Socialism, and Democracy*, 3rd ed., New York, Harper & Brothers, 1950.

A wide-ranging critique of both capitalism and socialism. Here the author summarizes his theory of the innovating role of the entrepreneur, and advances the notion that capitalism may be in more danger from its successes (particularly massive productive organizations) than from its failures.

WEBER, MAX: *The Theory of Social and Economic Organization*, New York, Oxford University Press, 1947.

Translation of the first part of a classic analysis of social economics. Talcott Parsons' introductory essay to the book is especially recommended.

WHYTE, WILLIAM FOOTE, ed.: *Industry and Society*, New York, McGraw-Hill Book Company, Inc., 1946.

A short book with very little use of technical terminology. Includes an outstanding essay by Allison Davis on "The Motivation of the Underprivileged Worker."